THE WORLD ACCORDING TO JACOB

THE WORLD ACCORDING TO JACOB

HILARIOUS WORDS OF WISDOM FROM A LITTLE OLD SOUL

JACOB AND DONNA WHELAN

Black&White

Black&White

First published in the UK in 2024 by
Black & White Publishing Ltd
Nautical House, 104 Commercial Street, Edinburgh, EH6 6NF

A division of Bonnier Books UK
4th Floor, Victoria House, Bloomsbury Square, London, WC1B 4DA
Owned by Bonnier Books
Sveavägen 56, Stockholm, Sweden

A CIP catalogue record for this book is available from the British Library.

ISBN: 9781 78530 693 8

1 3 5 7 9 10 8 6 4 2

Design by Richard Budd
Printed and bound in Great Britain by Clays Ltd, Elcograf S.p.A.

www.blackandwhitepublishing.com

We dedicate our book to our wonderful family and friends, and especially to all our followers that have supported us on our social media journey.

We have loved sharing our little family updates with you all and let's not forget Jacob's words of wisdom! It is so lovely to see all the comments and messages you guys leave – it brightens our day reading through those!

We thank you all from the bottom of our hearts.

Contents

A VERY IMPORTANT MESSAGE . . .

hello

FROM JACOB

Hi, it's me Jacob, I am inside the book! I can't wait to share all my thoughts, memories and stories with you all. Mostly, me and my Mammy came up with this. This is my first book, not even my second book or anything. I never wrote a book before but after seven years I am finally able to. It was sometimes in my dreams to write my very own book and I hope you have loads of wonderful laughs as you read it. I can't wait to show you all how I see the world through my eyes!

FROM DONNA

It is so wonderful that Jacob and I are writing this book together and it will be a great little memory to have and to look back on. Jacob brings so much joy to everyone who knows him, especially me, his Daddy Kevin and little sister Maisie. We are all so proud! I have recorded a lot of our chats and I am going to try my very best to share those and lots of other fun stuff with you in our very first book, The World According to Jacob.

Jacob: When was I born, in June?

Donna: You were born in June.

Jacob: Born in June? The same as my birthday!?

Donna: Yeah, that's why you have a birthday because that's when you were born.

Jacob: I am going to have a June birthday every single time? Every single week?

Donna: Every year! Your birthday is in June, is that crazy?

Jacob: Yeah!

1
WHEN WAS I BORN?

I was born on the 28th of June in 2017. My Mammy was the first person that I looked at and the first person that I loved! My Daddy was second but I love them the same now!

I started to talk from a very young age, do you know I was having conversations at two years old? My Mammy says I have not stopped talking ever since. A little old soul she says! Well. I love to talk and talk. I like to ask questions. It's how you find out about things, I like to wonder you know...

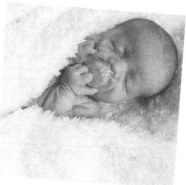

chat, chat, chat and more chat!!

You are always gonna be my Mammy, even when you're up in heaven!

Jacob

FAMILY

Okay, so let's begin with the most important thing in the whole wide world. And in the world according to me that has to be FAMILY!

I will tell you all about my family. There is my Mammy Donna, Daddy Kevin and my little sister Maisie, and then there is me, Jacob. We are all from Dublin, Ireland but I won't tell you all my address because, well, that's not safe. Mammy tells us we need to be careful about sharing that kind of thing. It's different from sharing toys, which she says I have to do. Especially with Maisie, but that's okay.

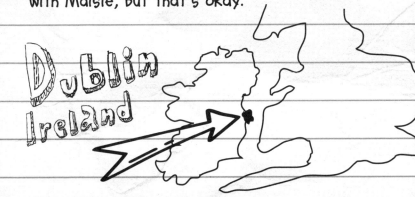

My little sister Maisie

I became a brother when I was three years old.
At first I said I don't want a sister or a girl,
but when Maisie came home from hospital, I was
jumping around. I could not hold my excitement in.
It was just bursting out of me!

Maisie was so small, like a little doll. You know,
like those baby Annabells
… yeah that's what she
was like. I gave her a little
smoochy-smooch and a lend
of my doggy teddy and I think
that's what made her like me
so much!

Maisie is three years old now. I like caring for her and teaching her stuff but sometimes she likes to do things her own way. You wouldn't want to hear her sometimes. I do sometimes have to tell her, "You can't do that Maisie!" She always says "sowy" and I say, "Maisie I am sorry too, okay baby," and we give each other a big hug and do you know what? She always tries to wiggle and run away!

I think Maisie loves me because I am a good brother. I help her with stuff and do everything for her, but she does not do everything for me sometimes, but I think it is funny!

Our favourite thing to do together is build forts. We always gather all the big blankets from around the house and all the cushions and pillows from the sofa.

I tell Maisie what to do so she can help me, so she hands me things that I need. When we have the fort built up with our secret tunnel to get to the inside we always ask my Mammy for a snack cos you know you get hungry after hard work building. We then like to chill out together and tell each other funny stories and have loads of giggles. My Mammy said it's okay to build forts as long as we help to clean up after but I don't mind that.

This week I have been helping Maisie learn how to count. Do you know she can count to thirteen now! And guess how I taught her – with a nice game of hide and seek. I always find the best spot but Maisie – I am shaking my head right now – she hides in the same spot all the time and you can see her as clear as anything. But do you know what I do? I pretend I can't see her, so I would be like,

"Oh, where could she be? Is she over here? Over there?"

And all you can hear is her laughing so loud! She always jumps out and says,

"Here I am!"

I definitely think she needs some practice with the hiding! She'll get the hang of it one day, I'm sure. Then it'll be even more fun!

Maisie loves me and kisses me on the cheek all the time. Her first favourite movie is Woody Woodpecker and the second one is Toy Story. She is cute, funny and just a little bit bossy, but most of all she is my sister and I love her!

My Daddy

My Daddy is the greatest! When I grow up
I want to be just like him. I love that he
shows me how I can do things. He is very
good at explaining in a way that I can always
understand.

We like to exercise together and keep fit
and look after our bodies. My Daddy says
exercising is not only good for your body but
also good for your mind. He is definitely right
because I always feel great after we go! I love
that we get to spend time together just the
two of us and we get some peace from the girls
hehehe.

I got a shiny golden bike from Santa this year,
it has black mag wheels and they are so cool.
They zoom in the wind and you should see how
fast I go!

My Daddy has a red fixie bike so we zoom
together when we go on our cycles. I have all
the gear to keep me safe, a golden helmet, knee
pads, arm pads and a bright yellow vest with a
star on it just in case it gets dark outside. I
still have to get the hang of the wheelies and
bunny hops on this bike because it is so much
more bigger than my last one!

Me and Daddy also like to build things together. We made a shed for our bikes and we made a plant box for my Nanny and Grandad. I was thinking of telling them a good spot where they could put it. Maybe they can put it on the window sill outside the back garden so the flowers can get some sun. I want to paint it rainbow colours for them so I just need to get some paint brushes first. I hope they like rainbows, but doesn't everyone?

Friday night is lads night. We always decide together what we should do. Sometimes we go out, maybe play some football or go on a drive and get a burger and watch the aeroplanes! Or sometimes we like to get pizza, play computer games and watch funny videos. We still haven't agreed with one thing and that is who is the GOAT (Greatest of All Time) in football. My Daddy says Messi, I say Ronaldo!

MAN CHAT iS BETWEEN THE LADS.

We always have the best laughs when we are together. He always tickles me, and I do be laughing so much I do think I need to wee!

My Mammy

As you probably know by now guys, one of my favourite things to do is talk! I like to have chats with my Mammy. We chat about anything and everything and I like that she always listens to me. I think it is very important to be able to talk with someone close to you and tell them your thoughts and feelings about things. I always start our conversations with, "So how was your day Mammy?" As easy as that, and then we're off with our chat!

My favourite time to chat to my Mammy is just before bed because everything always comes to my head at night time and sometimes I even get to stay up an extra few minutes! We always make each other laugh until our bellies hurt. Even if she gives out sometimes, I know she is just looking out for me. She is a great Mammy, she looks after us very good and she always makes me feel safe, I just love her so much.

Family time

I do like getting out and about with my family but I also like doing little things like getting in to my Mammy and Daddy's bed, the four of us just chilling out and watching movies and best of all with a big load of sweets!

It's okay to have sweets every now and then guys, okay? Eating healthy is important but eating sweets is important too!

If I could choose another family I wouldn't change it — I love mine!

I think I make a lot of people laugh even when I am not telling jokes and I'm just talking. I don't really know why. My Mammy says it is because I am being my happy self. I do get sad sometimes like when my goldfish Bob died but he is in fishy heaven now, swimming around up there, so that cheers me up!

3

LIFE

Do you ever wonder why we are on this planet? Well, I think our life is made out of memories.

Do you ever get a memory stuck in your head?

The best fun days

I have a lot of fun memories. One of my favourite memories so far is that I was visiting Cork with my family and our friends during the summer holidays. We rented a house out for the weekend, we went to the zoo down there and I got to see a big giraffe. He even smiled for a photo for my Daddy! We had so much fun just being all together. The weather was so good and the sun was shining down.

On the way back from our trip we decided to stop into Tramore at the funfair. There was this big water boat rollercoaster. Well, I decided to go on it with my Mammy and you should have seen my face – it was so funny! I am dreaming of going back there and doing that again!

My favourite days are the summer days. Cos you know why? You just get out, get fresh air and when it is all sunny out you can go places, go on adventures. Sometimes you might just go somewhere and have a big fun party outside or you might even have a picnic. Doing those sorts of things is the best!

Dream a little dream

So let's chat about our feelings and dreams. I love dreams!

Did you ever have a dream that you were rich? And you had enough money and you were chilling in your dream and you wake up and you are awake in your actual life? And you say this is not my mansion? Is my Ferrari outside? No it was a dream!

I had a cool dream that it was raining and I could pick what it was raining! I would pick all food that is tasty and wish there was glass plates that can never break and it will just land and it won't even get dirty. I'd pick all food that exists because I'd eat anything!

I had another dream that everything can walk and when I just tried to get something it just ran away! It just runs away and I go to get it again and it runs away, go to get it again, just runs away. I go to get the PlayStation controller and it just runs out of my hand and lands on the chair! Then there was a blanket on the bottom that jumps down and runs around the place and I'm like, "I can't find anything in this house!" Then I woke up picked up the remote and I was like,

it was a dream!

I love having dreams — it's like it's real life!

MY FAVOURITE FOOD

I love burgers and a cheese pizza and I can't forget about going to the pub for some pub grub. I get bacon, cabbage, mashed potatoes, carrots, stuffing and roast potatoes, with gravy on top. Yummy!

My favourite sweets are jellies and ice pops.

New things

Trying something new can feel scary, like the time I took my stabilisers off my bike. It just came to my head and I thought to myself, "Alright, I am ready to learn how to cycle."

I made a plan that I was going to practise on the grass so I wouldn't take that much damage if I fell. At first I cried, I wanted to put them back on but my Mammy and Daddy reminded me of what I said, "You can do this Jacob!"

So I hopped on, at first I was a bit wobbly, the bike fell down ... but it didn't hurt so I was like okay ... I can do this and I did it because I believed in myself!

You will always be brave when you say "I can do this" three times in your head!

Dance – you can do it!

I was just five years old when I started my classes of dancing, singing and acting. We were all practising very hard for like six months for our show. I had a little script to learn and everything. It was my first ever time to be on a big stage. I was feeling a little nervous but do you know what I done, I said,

"I can do this"

three times in my head like this:

"I can do this, I can do this, I can do this."

And guess what? I did it! It is a great feeling when you conquer those nerves and be proud of yourself.

You can dance if you want to!

If you are trying to do something new, you should try this. It works!

You will always be brave if you tell yourself you can do this three times in your head!

It's okay to be not okay!

If I was having a bad day I would actually tell somebody that's close to me. Yeah I would do that, I would tell somebody close. Why would you keep it to yourself though? If you do that guys, then remember that:

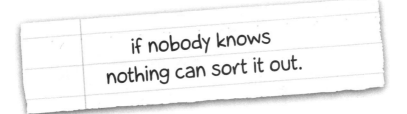

if nobody knows
nothing can sort it out.

Like if you are a kid you can tell an adult and you could probably go somewhere and it might turn into a good day! Always tell somebody close to you!

Calm mode!

Keep calm and take a breath

Apart from lifting weights, do you know what calms me down? It's if you breathe ten times. So you do this:

breathe in through your nose, then

take a big breath out from your mouth.

It's easy, so go on, just try it there. Did that calm you down?

More best days

Sometimes I want to be invincible and free, but sometimes I want to stay inside like if I was all relaxed on the chair. I like having those days too!

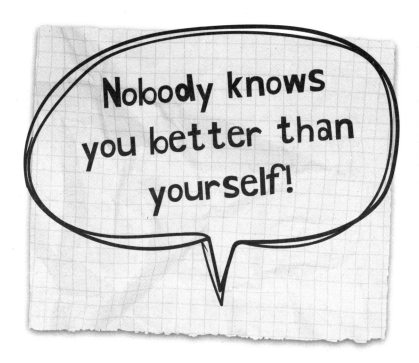

There is so much that I love about my life, my family, friends and food that people make! Thanks to everyone that makes it, especially picnic food as I love being outside in the park with my family getting fresh air.

I like having a good life in my house or getting out in the back garden, jumping on the trampoline, or going out on my bike to get exercise with my Daddy. I just feel free, you know? When you just cycle only around a road or in a cul-de-sac that's kinda boring for me.

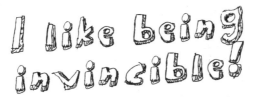

4

ADVENTURE

My favourite days are the summer days. You just get out, get fresh air, when it's all sunny you can get out somewhere and go on adventures and maybe even have a little picnic.

I like to go different places, somewhere you have never been, cos you know why? You get to explore somewhere new! And there's nothing more exciting than new stuff. Toys, people, places, whatever! And there is so much to see and do all you need to do is find them. You don't want to be stuck doing the same old stuff, day after day. Who wants that? That's just **BORING!**

Ireland is very beautiful and I love living here! I have visited a good few places so let me tell you a few of my favourites.

Dublin City

I love the Spire – it's huge. It goes right up to the sky! I do have to bend my head right back to look up at it. It's SO tall! I like walking down along O'Connell Street, holding my sister's hand when we go, because it can get very busy! You can just see everybody going about their business in there!

Then there's the GPO. And the Ha'penny Bridge – now that's a very old bridge which is two hundred years old! Can you believe that?

I wonder what they did in the olden days when they wanted to get from one side of the river to the other but nobody had bothered to build a bridge? Did they just swim across? I don't think I'd like to do that in the winter time – it would be freezing! We should talk about the weather in Ireland. Sometimes it rains so much it looks like you've been out for a swim!

Underneath the bridge you can see the River Liffey just floating along. I suppose it's been doing that for a really long time. I think maybe they built their own little boats just paddling along the River Liffey. Maybe they gave other people a lift across if they needed it.

Facts are real life. It's not a story or a fairytale.

And on top of the bridge there is a very beautiful view of the city when you stand on your tiptoes. That's something grown-ups don't think about so much when they say, "Will you look at that!" Some of us are a bit smaller and can't see what they're on about! I do be like, "Lift me up and show me!"

I was walking by Temple Bar a while ago and got a bubble-gum flavour ice-cream just outside. You do see lots of people there going in to drink Guinness around there! My Daddy likes a pint of Guinness when he goes on a night out to the pub! Don't ya Daddy!

There is lots of places to visit in Dublin City.
It's especially good on St Patrick's Day because
there is a big parade and loads of people from
all around the world come to watch it! Everyone
wears something green, funny hats and wigs,
and you can't forget about some shamrocks and
waving the flags! It's so fun.

I like going to the Phoenix Park – it's very big
and it's good if you like a nice walk or a cycle.
You see a lot of people keeping fit there. You
can see the Wellington Monument too and Pope's
Cross and even deers live there! And there is
also Dublin Zoo and best of all, a playground!

I love lighthouses and if you like those there is a really nice one called Poolbeg! It has a lovely walk along up to it and you can just see the big ferries coming in and out. And it's red – my favourite colour!

I also like going to Howth too. It's really nice in the evenings, when the sun goes down, just walking along looking at the boats and it has a playground beside it too, wink wink! And if you walk all the way down the pier (if you're a kid you have to hold your mammy or daddy's hand and be very careful), anyways around the corner there is another lighthouse, it feels very peaceful when you go there just looking out at the sea. Perfect after a day running around.

In Wexford, Courtown is fun. I like going to the carnival and the arcades there and the beach. It's a great place to go in the summer days as there is so much to do!

Bray is brilliant when the air show is on and you can see all the planes doing tricks and loop the loops! I even seen red, yellow and blue smoke coming out of them when I was there. They were making love hearts in the sky with the planes! I remember just chilling with my sister eating a big ice-cream looking up and saying to myself, "How do they do that?!"

I like to visit petting farms and seeing all the animals. I like giving breadcrumbs to the ducks and carrots to the goats. They do be running over to you sticking their heads out of the fence to see who can get one first! In some of these farms you can even hold snakes and tarantulas. My sister Maisie got to do that in playschool but nope, not for me – no way Jose!

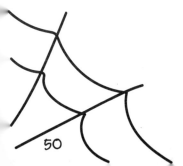

Holiday, holiday, I need a holiday!

Last year we went on a holiday to Albufeira in Portugal. When I got on the aeroplane I was slapping my face to see if it was real or if I was dreaming! Did that ever happen to you? That something so good was happening and you just couldn't believe it! It's a great feeling to get.

I loved going to the beach with my family making sandcastles, the sun just shining down on us nice and warm! I kept going over with my Mammy to the sea, catching the water from the little waves in my bucket. It was just so peaceful and happy just being there, the four of us all together.

We don't get as many of those sunny days in Ireland like some other countries do but when we do we make the most of it! When the sun's out we go straight out that door!

Like I said before, it rains a lot a lot in Ireland, but I remember this one day my Mammy and Daddy said, "Put on your wellies and let's just go out." We brought our umbrellas and put our big coats on. I saw the biggest puddle and ran through it and that was so fun! Maisie followed me in and the two of us were just jumping around and dancing and singing in the rain. Mammy said that was an old film title, and a song. I think she maybe even sang it but I can't remember how it went. Maisie ended up falling in the puddle on her butt and we were all just laughing so hard and she got muck all over her! She was covered in it. Sometimes that sort of fun is the best when you just laugh and laugh and laugh till your stomach hurts.

I do like getting out and about with my family but I also like doing little things, like when it's raining outside, just getting into my Mammy and Daddy's bed, the four of us just chilling out and watching movies and best of all with a big load of sweets!

Some things I like

Adventures are fun, I like to run in the sun

I like to see the animals and everything outside . . .

I like to see trees and I like the sound of the cheeping little birds

I like my t-shirt flowing around in the breeze and I like visiting new places and seeing new things

But most of all, I always try to remember that

Life is just one big adventure,

where you can go wherever you want!

5

KINDNESS

Be kind guys! Just make sure to be kind – that's when you'll feel even more better and have an even better day!

i'm expectin that loveliness in ya!

jacob

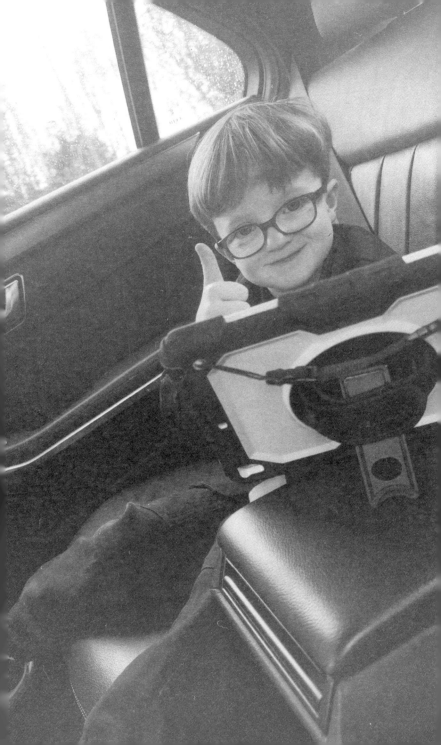

Money, money, money

Every week I do little chores around the house
to help my Mammy and Daddy and on Fridays I
get pocket money. I was saving up for a while
and I had fifty euro altogether – not bad, eh? I
had my eye on this very cool case for my tablet.
It's lime green and it has a cool twisty thing
at the back so it can stand up. My other one
broke and so I needed a new one. I like to stand
my tablet up at the kitchen table to watch or
listen to my music playlist when I have a snack
after school and sometimes I sneak it into the
bathroom while I do a number two! Hehehe!

I wanted a new case for a while so I got my Daddy to order me it. I had been using anything that I could find in the kitchen to stand it up, like bottles of water and even the bottle of tomato ketchup. That worked fine but it was time I got a new one. So that was twenty-five euro, which is a lot of money. I always hear grown-ups saying things about how important it is to save and not just spend, but when you're a kid you sometimes just need to get stuff you want, especially if no one is offering to get it for you! Grown-ups might offer to get you something like a new case for your tablet but maybe not the one you really want, when the one you REALLY want is THE COOL ONE!

Always put the biggest number in your head first and then count on!

Number bonds

You can use number bonds to help you work out all the pairs of numbers that add up to the same total.

For example
$3 + 7 = 10$ and $7 + 3 = 10$
$4 + 6 = 10$ and $6 + 4 = 10$

These number bonds all add up to a total of either 10 or 20. Fill in the missing numbers.

$1 + \boxed{} = 10$ $14 + \boxed{} = 20$

$4 + \boxed{} = 10$ $\boxed{} + 6 = 20$

$\boxed{} + 9 = 10$ $18 + \boxed{} = 20$

$7 + \boxed{} = 10$ $\boxed{} + 3 = 20$

$\boxed{} + 7 = 10$ $11 + \boxed{} = 20$

$6 + \boxed{} = 10$ $\boxed{} + 4 = 20$

$\boxed{} + 10 = 20$

$3 + \boxed{} = \boxed{}$

Toy story

After he'd ordered it for me I went into my
Daddy when he was chilling on the sofa and I
asked him if we could all go on a spin in the car
to the shops so I could spend the rest. So we
all hopped in the car. I had my wallet and all
with me, ready to rock!

We decided to stop off at the discount shop
because you can get loads of bits and bobs in
there. I picked up the little piece to add to my
pump for my ball. That cost two euro and was
handy as my basketball was after going down so
I definitely needed one of those! So now I was
up to twenty-seven.

Then I spotted a big huge water gun and, oh well, I needed that, even though the sun wasn't out yet. But then I thought to myself, sure I will have it for when the sun is out. And I was thinking, I could even just spray the walls or clean the garden with it or ... ooooh GOOD IDEA, water my Nanny's plants! Do you think she would let me?

Right so that was that. I was getting it. And it was only nine euro so that just hopped in my basket! Ha-ha! So what am I on now? Oh yeah, thirty-six!

I could hear Maisie shout, "Dinosaur!" She was after spotting a big orange dinosaur sitting on the shelf and it cost nine euro. I could get her that. I had enough money. So I said, "Let's get it Maisie!" and you should have seen her face – she had the biggest smile!

My Mammy said that she would pay for Maisie but I just told her, "It's okay, I've got it!" We both went up to the till together wheeling our baskets. We took our stuff out and handed it to the lady and she said that will be twenty euro please so I took my money from my wallet and paid.

I handed Maisie her dinosaur. She was so happy and so was I because I had a fiver left that will get us an ice-cream later from the ice-cream man!

Tooth fairy

Im expecting
that loveLiness
in ye

from Jacob
XOXOXOXOXOX

OUR
FAMILY
20!

We skipped back to the car together. I was feeling very happy with myself and after that my Mammy and Daddy told me that I did a very kind thing and that made me feel proud.

It's a good feeling you get when you be kind.

And on top of that, do you know working out how much of your pocket money you're spending is a great way to practise adding up your numbers! Must remember to tell my teacher I've been practising!

School buddies

I am in first class so today junior infants came over to our class and teacher said we had to pick a partner. I teamed up with a little girl. She was five years old, so a year younger than me. We read some books and did some maths games, we found some rhyming words, we played with play-doh, I helped her and she even helped me.

We then went to the PE hall to do some exercising. We had so much fun, and then the kids from junior infants had to try to get the ball from us kids in first class, but I went easy on the junior infants and I just let her win all the time! It's a good feeling to let others win sometimes because then it makes them happy!

Sometimes I wonder why would you want to make someone feel bad? What is the point of that? You should help people out when you can. Think about how they would feel if you were mean – it would make them very sad, wouldn't it?

You know like when someone makes a joke thinking they are funny and the other person is not laughing. You just have to be careful with your words and not hurt anybody's feelings.

I like doing kind things for my family and friends, like that time I was with my auntie and a lady dropped her money on the floor and I picked it up and gave it to her! And you know what she done? She ended up giving me loads of coins and I was saying, "No, you keep it it's yours!" and she said, "No, you can keep it!" Which just goes to show that:

You should always do the right thing!

You can also show kindness on birthdays and all pick out special things that you think the person would like. My Daddy's birthday is coming up so I have been saving my pocket money and I'm thinking of doing a special surprise for him on our next lads night when it's just the two of us.

I think he would like that!

6

CELEBRATION

As I mentioned before, my birthday is in June. This year it landed on the last day of school before we finished up for the summer.

I said, "Mammy, I just want a day off."

And she says, "Jacob, you say this every year. Why do you think you should have a day off?"

I said, "Mammy, it's the last day of school!"

And she said, "Yeah, it's the last day of school for two months – you don't need a day off!"

Well I said, "I do ... an extra day off is better than nothing!"

I had a feeling I'm not getting the day off – birthday or no birthday!

But with my birthday being at the same time every year, as I said earlier, I'll ask again next year and see what happens. As my Nanny Lisa keeps saying:

GOD LOVES A TRIER

So I'll have another try next year! And the year after that. And maybe the year after that too...

Remember to always try your best!

Festival fun

I'm gonna go to a festival next year. It has music, a funfair and loads of activities and I'm camping at it so that will be fun, and there's a big gang of us going. I can't wait!

My Nanny Lisa and Granda Richie are coming too and they have a campervan! How cool is that?

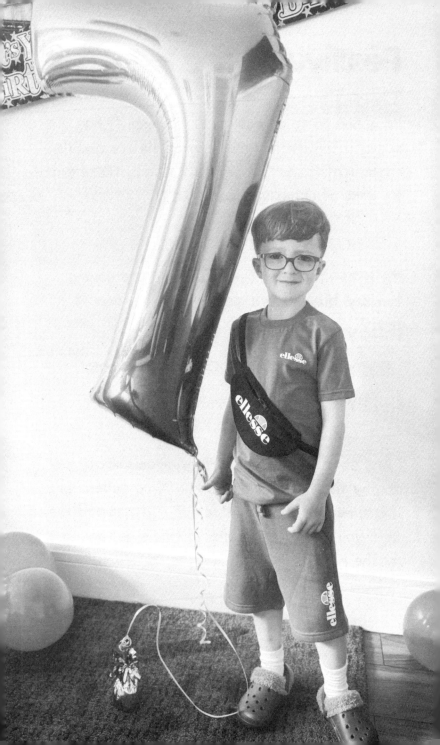

Birthdays are a Big Deal

Birthdays are so fun because you get to celebrate your life with the people closest to you. Birthdays are a day that's special just for you, so I always sing:

Happy birthday to me!
Happy birthday to me!
Happy birthday toooooo meeeeee
Happy birthday to me!

I was six and three-quarters when I wrote this and by the time you read this I'll be seven. Or if you read this after I've had another birthday then you'll need add more years to get my age. At the moment I'm getting close to seven!

Every year my Nanny Maro [Mary] always says she is twenty-one and in my head I'm like, "Yeah, right Nanny – that just doesn't add up." Maybe she just forgot, hee hee hee.

It's Christmas!

I love Christmas time! I wonder what I will get from Santa this year?

So every year on Christmas Eve I go to my Nanny Lisa's and Granda Richie's for a party with my cousins. My Nanny gets us all matching Christmas pyjamas and we give each other presents and sing and dance and have lots of sweets.

I am the oldest and only grandson on my Mammy's side of the family. I have all girl cousins – Keeva, Saoirse, Mya and Maddie – and I also have an auntie Leah who is three years older than me! And then there are my other aunties Edel and Shan Abbie and Carlie.

My Nanny Lisa always tells me I'm her favourite grandson!

Last year, we all sat together on the stairs for some Christmas photos. It took ages for all the little ones to look at the camera! I was like, "Hurry up get me outta here – I want to party!" I think we are going to do that again this year and I'm hoping it's quicker than last year's!

I do be so excited for Christmas Eve with all my family. I just love that feeling you get Christmas morning running down the stairs to see what Santa left and giving each other the special Christmas gifts we bought!

We always have the best time together at Nanny's house and what's great about going there is they always gives us nice things. She always has orange juice for me and ice pops. We all just run in and grab everything when we visit! I also like the summer time there cos they have a big back garden and we have BBQs and have lots of fun together.

Da's Ma and Da

On my Daddy's side of the family, myself and Maisie are the only grandchildren. My Granda Tomo is my best bud – he always says that to me. When we go over there Nanny Maro and Granda always have jellies ready for me and chocolate bars for Maisie.

They have two dogs, Trigger and Jessie, and every time we pull up they do be barking so loud and running out to see us. Trigger is getting older now and a little bit slower and he only has three legs! I always run in and give him a rub when I see him!

My Granda always walks out to the car when we are going home and my Nanny Maro sits in the porch waving. He always tickles me and Maisie through the window when we get strapped into the car!

I am very lucky to have a great family to celebrate all the different occasions with.

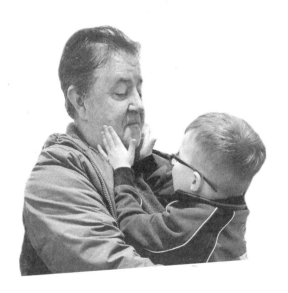

I Love the Movies!

Recently I went for an audition for a movie and I got picked! I was hoping I would because I had a feeling they liked me because they were just smiling the whole entire time.

I am in a stage school over a year now and I really enjoy it!

It was my first time to do anything like this and I had to go for a lot of auditions for the part. My Mammy helped me to prepare for that and we practised very hard! I'm probably going to have a lot of auditions during my life if I do acting so it was fine if I didn't get it.

When I got the call to tell me I did, I was screaming so loud! I rang all my family to tell them and they were just so happy for me. I can't wait for the movie to come out. And honestly, it's just like that feeling I get when I'm going on holiday. I really can't believe it but:

I'm gonna be a Mooooooovie Star!

Oh to be
a star!

7
FRIENDSHIP & SCHOOL

Friends are great because if you fall they will help you up!

hello

Apart from my family I have made loads of friends in my life. I like when you meet a new friend and you play with them. It's so fun and then when you go to play with them again it's familiar and you have an even better time.

I recently made a new friend in school – do you know what I did? I just went up to him, asked his name and said hey do you want to be friends? And he said sure and we have been playing in the yard together all week! SIMPLE AS THAT!

I will tell you a funny story, one day I was playing at the playground and I went up to this boy and I said hey do you want to be friends? I was wearing my Liverpool jersey and do you know what he said? Yes, I will, but only if you support Man United as well. I pointed at the Liverpool crest on my jersey and said, "What's this look like? I'm sticking to my team!" He end up chasing me around then!

I have a friend Indi. We met in junior infants nearly four years ago now and we have been playing ever since. I think we are going to last forever! I always run to her and jump in her arms and Indi is strong, I tell you! She can lift me up no problem! Well, she is taller than me.

I like that we stick up for each other and we can tell each other things and make each other laugh. We always be crazy when we get together and just have the best time. I like that we can also chat to each other, I like that she cares for me and I care for her cos that's what friends are for!

You be kind

You stick up for each other

You laugh

You be crazy

You play

You have fun

When they cry you find a way to make them laugh

And you pick each other up when you fall

(or go tell teacher)

School

Talking of school, which I do quite a lot of, I'll start off with what I do like about it. And that is — I like learning new things!

Well I've realised now that I love maths and it is my favourite. I can count more than my ten fingers now and I can remember sums. I have a good memory! I have got so much better at it since I started junior infants.

I like to do my rough work like at the side of the page to show teacher how I worked the sum out!

Hocus Pocus,
Time to
Focus!

I also like building things with Lego and getting creative. I love playing sports like basketball, football, rugby and tennis.

I like playing with all my friends in the yard making up our own games. I have even made friends with kids in other classes and I get to play with them in the yard and have lots of fun.

And I love our school trips. On the last one we went on a big bus and I got to sit beside my friend Mark. He always cracks me up – we always laugh when we are together. Sometimes in class we have to get separated from each other because we just make each other laugh a bit too much!

On our last trip we went on a lovely nature walk in the Wicklow mountains and played some arts and crafts. I got to write a story about a little monkey.

This is how it went...

A monkey brang up a towel and put the towel up on the tree, jumped into the sea from the top and then he swam back to shore, he climbed back up the tree got the towel climbed back down the tree, went inside dried himself and then he got changed into clothes. Then he had some lunch and then he had dinner and then he decided to jump back in the sea again!

The end [story by Jacob]

I liked writing this story, using my imagination. I had a good laugh to myself while I wrote it! I hope the monkey did too! Sounds like a perfect fun day to me.

I like to do all the class activities, the fun stuff!

I sometimes find reading and spellings a little hard. I am going to work on that better this year.

Movement breaks – ah, I am not the biggest fan! I don't mind a little few but when it is first thing in the morning and I am only awake, I do be saying in my head like teacher can you calm the ham!

1 + 2 =

I love when it is home time and my Mammy and Maisie collect me and I always run around with my friends Alanna and Charlie to get my bike from the shed.

I do let them take a turn up to the gate before I go my way home. I don't mind sharing with them, they do be like it's my turn, then I do have to say you go first and then you go second and switch it around the following day ... oh these girls!

I like giving Maisie a hug and asking her how was her day at playschool. I can't wait until she goes to my school. Then maybe I could drop her to her class and that would be good.

I like telling my Mammy about my day on the way back to my house.

I love when I get home and I get out of my uniform and put something comfy on, get a snack and just chill out for a while in peace!

I miss my family when I am in school – it does be good to get home!

i'm not going to school, i'm sick tomorrow. the doctor told me i'm sick tomorrow!

8
THERE'S LOTS OF LIFE STUFF TO THINK ABOUT!

As I'm starting to get a bit older – I'm seven now! – I realise that life isn't always as simple as it used to be, like in playschool. Here's some of the things I think about a bit more now. Maybe you think about them too?

Imagination

I like to use my imagination. I use it all the time.
I like that you can just think of anything you
want.

If I'm with my friends in the yard we use our
imaginations and it makes the games much more
fun! We made up a game in the yard called duck
tag so when somebody ducks you're safe but you
can only stay down for twenty seconds – any
longer than that you can be caught!

I think imagination is kind of like dreaming only you can control it.

Sometimes your imagination comes to life, like when I was imagining that I would be on an aeroplane and then I actually went on one! And I wasn't just dreaming it!

Well I do know that maybe I cannot really jump miles up into the sky or fly but there are some things I can do if I just put my mind to it and so can you!

Don't worry!
Be happy!

Worrying

When I started school I was so worried about leaving my Mammy I had my arms and legs wrapped around hers. I just felt so worried that I was starting something new it felt scary, but as time went on I got to make new friends, learned new things and played out in yard! It wasn't all that bad.

I still worry sometimes doing new things and meeting new people. Believe it or not, I can be shy sometimes but once the first few minutes are over and I get comfortable I am just fine!

Before I get older and have to worry about taxes, paying rent or buying your house, having bills and getting money out of the bank you have to pay, or worrying about holidays – until then I am going to chill and relax baby!!

What's the point in worrying about the little things? It is gonna be alright! Just like that Bob Marley song where he's singing don't worry about anything cos every little thing is gonna be alright! That's what I think anyway.

Patience

As you know I do chores and so I get pocket money for that and sometimes I ask my Nanny Lisa if she would like me to do some jobs for her and she pays me!

I decide each week what I am going to spend it on like sweets from the shop, a game on my tablet or a toy I am thinking about getting.

When I save up all my money for something that I want I can then go and spend it.

I am realising now how expensive things are so now I am really thinking do I really want it? Is it worth it?

Well, I tell you, it is easier for my Mammy and Daddy to just buy things for me than spending my own!

I love when someone buys me something and I didn't expect it. I got new earphones for my birthday but the sad thing is I ended up losing them. I was so angry and upset because they were really special to me.

I left them in my zip pocket and I forgot to zip it up! Next time I will have to give them to my Mammy to mind or make sure the zip is up! But lucky enough I had some birthday money so I was able to go and get some more. I also bought my sister Maisie a new teddy! Twenty-two euro it cost me! I was like, she is lucky to have a brother like me! It made me happy to be able to buy her something. Maisie has been sleeping with her new teddy every night – I just knew she would love it!

I am now learning that if you want something you can't just get it straight away you have to wait some time before you can get it, it is hard to wait but sometimes you just have to have a little bit of patience!

Live in the moment

Thankfulness

I am very thankful for my life and all the stuff
I have. I am thankful for my parents, my friends
and all my family. I thank God for all that stuff
too.

I am very thankful and I appreciate everything
I have in my life. I am lucky to have a home. Do
you know there is a lot of people homeless in
Ireland and all around the world and it's very
sad. I really hope one day in my life that I can
help. Everyone deserves a happy home and a
happy life. I wish a Happy Life to everyone.

Laughing

If you were crying would you feel good? Nope, but if you were laughing would you feel good? Yes, you would – that's why it is so good to laugh!

Everyone says I have a funny laugh – I just can't help it! If I find something funny, I will just keep thinking and thinking about it and I just can't stop – sometimes I can't even breathe! Did that ever happen to you?

If someone's upset I always try my best to make them laugh. I hate to see anyone cry! I like to make others laugh – it's a good feeling to be able to do that.

I'm wondering why you laugh when you get tickles? How does that happen?

133

Music

Listening to my favourite songs always cheers me up. If you are feeling sad then maybe you could listen to yours but I will tell you a few of mine right now:

Imagine Dragons: 'Bones', 'It's Ok' and 'Believer'

Bob Marley: 'Buffalo Soldier' and 'Three Little Birds (Everything's Gonna Be Alright)'

Benson Boone: 'Beautiful Things'

Noah Kahan: 'Stick Season'

Lukas Graham: '7 Years'

Tom Odell: 'Another Love'

Gotye (feat. Kimbra): 'Somebody That I Used to Know'

Rema: 'Calm Down'

Dermot Kennedy: 'Kiss Me'

Hozier: 'Too Sweet'

Calvin Harris: 'My Way'

Music always makes me feel happy when I am down!

Looking after your body!

I like to exercise because that's looking after your body and it's very good to look after your body! You can do exercise in loads of ways, like in school playing sports, playing tag with your friends, walking, swimming, dancing. There are loads of fun ways to exercise!

For the last while now I have started to go on cycles with my Daddy on the weekends. When we get up we have our breakfast, grab everything we need in our backpacks, put our safety gear on and go! Sometimes we put our bikes in the car and drive to different places to cycle.

I love it just being out and free. I used to be only able to cycle so far and I would be tired but with lots of practice now I can go for ages! I can do no handers on my bike and all!

Sometimes we even bring the football and we go to the Astro pitch and kick the ball about. The last time we went on a cycle we just got to the Astro pitch and it started to rain so we said, "Ah well, we will still play anyway." We were gonna be soaked either way if we cycled back. We had so much fun playing in the rain.

When we got back I went in to my Mammy and I was soaked. My glasses were all steamed up from the rain but I didn't care. My Mammy was like, "Let's take them wet clothes off," and she got my nice warm pyjamas for me! We didn't let a little rain ruin our fun!

I eat healthy, I eat all my vegetables like broccoli, carrots and cabbage, but sweets are good too every now and then!

I love burgers, they are my favourite food. My least favourite food is tuna. Don't know why, I just don't like it. In fact, between you and me, I hate it, it's disgusting, yuck! I'm just not a big fan of it!

I am even stronger now I have big muscley legs and arms because I exercise and I look after my body. I like to exercise – it just makes me happy!

I'm STILL wondering why you laugh when you get tickles? How does that happen?

9
BE ALL
YOU
CAN BE

I think we all have stuff we'd like to be better at or things we wish we could do. But you know what? We can't be great at everything and there are some things that, even if we try really hard, we just probably don't like it as much as other stuff. That's life! But if we do things and try our best at everything we do then we will find what we do like and also what we're good at, and, most importantly, we'll find the things that make us happy!

When I look at myself I'm big! No matter what anyone else tells me!

Try your best

You can do anything if you just try your best.

Ya know what? I was playing basketball the other day and I didn't get the first shot but then, at the second try, I won and I scored a basket!

You don't give up, you keep going! It's not the end of your life if ya don't get it the first time, you can try again like me!

Try, try
and TRY
AGAIN!!

Be yourself

Be yourself is what my family always says.
Nobody's the same. I repeat, nobody's the same.
You need to be yourself, ya know why? Cos you
are the only one that is like you and you're
unique. Everybody's unique and there is not
even one person that is not unique!

I like being me. I like everything about myself
and there is nothing to be unhappy about.
My body is so healthy and good, which I'm so
thankful for, and I love my life and my family.

I don't do everything everybody else does like if they are doing something. And if I don't like it, I just don't do it!

I am here on earth because I am special. Humans are special! I got made in 2017, and I am one of a kind. There is no one else like me and I like being myself and then it's up to other people if they want to hang around with me or be my friend. It's great if they do but fine if they don't. They need to be themselves too!

You are special and you are supposed to be here because you can look after the earth. You are so special, nobody is specialer than humans not even a 100 billion trillion quadrillion cars! Humans are specialer than everything!

10
THE FUTURE

I think about the future a lot. What will it be like when I am older? I wonder what I will work as? I wonder what my house is going to look like or what car I have? I wonder what Maisie will be doing? I wonder if I am going to have the same friends or if I will make new ones? I wonder what adventures me and my family will have together? I wonder what places I will visit? I wonder will we discover aliens on a different planet – the universe is infinity long I reckon? I really wonder how my life is going to be? It is already exciting. I can't wait to see what the future brings for me! I think if you do good, good things will happen!

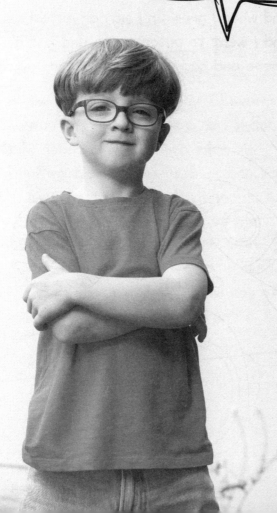

Earth and Outer Space

Here's a story about me, Jacob, and one of my dreams:

Once upon a time I was just pretending to be an astronaut and when I grew up I was an actual astronaut and I went to outer space and had a little home there and had so much fun.

It was a little home on the moon!

And guess what? There was air that could be released into it and there was no chimney! I just travelled up there to sleep and watch movies, eating my popcorn and living my life! I just went there to chill on my own with my space rocket!

I wonder how long it takes to go around the earth in a space rocket? I suppose it would depend how far away you are from the earth or how close you are! If you can see blue you are definitely close to the earth!

You can help the earth by not littering, you could pick up the trash if you see it. Maybe you could put a hi-vis jacket on and have a bin and a grabber! That would be good. You can't just throw rubbish on the ground or the grass, you are living on earth! It has gravity and life on it! It is special, maybe aliens are living on a different planet that hasn't even been discovered yet! Everyone should look after earth – it is a very special place so it is!

I think if aliens really came to visit us then that's what they'd say: "Guys, you've got a beautiful little planet here – but you do need to look after it like we do ours." (Theirs is probably spotless!)

Future me

I went to my first music festival this year when I turned the big seven with my family and I loved it. I can't wait until I do it again, maybe in the future. I could see some of my favourite singers on stage and that would be so cool!

I want to get a phone when I am a teenager and walk home from school by myself!

Well, it is fun to be a kid learning and all like in school. I like maths the best and what I hear from my Mammy and Daddy is that it is not actually as fun being a grown-up! Sometimes I think to myself, "Come on life, go quicker!"

I am probably going to be a movie actor. Maybe I will be in some scary movies, or funny ones if that doesn't work out. Maybe I could be in a circus, you know, like one of those that does the hat tricks.

I would like to have some more fun with my family and I would also like to do good stuff with my family in the future because when I'm grown up I might not be living with them anymore but I will have my own house and maybe I can still go on holidays with my family! That would be fun.

I would like to have loads of good cars, big cool ones like a Bugatti or a Lamborghini!

I would also love to be a designer of a house or maybe design my own house! It would be four storeys and I would have triangle windows in the attic and even solar panels! I would probably have a two-storey front door! It would be made out of obsidian! That would cost millions of euro! And the door handle would be metal!

My family can come stay over in the attic. I am joking! That's where my gym is going to be! I'm going to have a little balcony on my house and also a big swimming pool with a slide that goes down into it! There's going to be shelter that goes over it and rain covers that you can pull over and I'll be saying when it's raining that I am going swimming and people be like, "Are you mad?" But there is going to be shelter!

I'm going to have a race track out my back garden for my cars and bikes and it's gonna be a lovely modern house!

I am the big seven now. I wonder what it's going to be like this year and what is going to happen? I can't wait to make loads more friends and have lots of fun memories with my family and go on loads of adventures!

Maybe I'll just stick to having fun for now and we'll just have to wait and see what the future looks like when it happens!

THANK YOU . . .

We would like to thank Andrea Roche Agency for helping us to find the amazing team at Black & White Publishing. A special thank you to Ali, Thomas and the team – we are forever grateful for all your help with achieving the very best book for Jacob. We could not be happier with how it has all come together! Thank you to all our supportive family, friends and followers – we appreciate you all!

IMAGE CREDITS

All photographs courtesy of Donna Whelan, except for those listed below which are copyright © Sean Cahill 2024.
Pages: vi, viii, 2, 5, 16 (middle), 19, 20, 26, 36, 38, 41, 42, 58, 60, 81, 97, 112, 117, 127, 128, 130, 141, 142, 146, 150, 152 and 164

DONNA WHELAN

Born in Dublin, Ireland, I am a proud mother to Jacob and
Maisie. I first started sharing videos of Jacob during Covid
and never expected them to go so far! I enjoy every moment
of sharing our family adventures with you all. You may not see
me much, but I am behind the camera doing all the work!
(Just joking). I love capturing as much as I can so I will never
forget all these lovely memories that we have shared together
so far. Jacob, I will always be your No.1 supporter as well as
Maisie and Daddy Kevin. We are so proud of you!

@keepupwithjacob on TikTok
@donna_jacobs_mammy on Instagram